Psychology of Thinking

Thinking

1

The Collective
of Poems

This book is for anyone who can see, through these poems the very nature and beauty of everyday items and of nature, it's self, that is all around us. Let me, take you on a journey to explore the atoms of thought; on how we can view and understand our fascinating world, we live in; in way you never have seen before. This collection of poetry was written between 1977, when I wrote my very first poem, in the classroom, where my fellow class mates and I had our finished work's publish in a small book, call; Opinions, to this very day in 2015.

The Seagulls

Dashing, round under trees,
with red, little feet
and small brown beaks.
Grey feathered friends,
scavenge for food.
Round,
tables and chairs.
Scurry, scurry,
scurrying,
for food!

Summer Days

Summer days, down by the sea.
Towels stretched out,
on the sand.
Many hats, scattered,
along the shore.
Board-shorts, surfing,
amongst the waves.
Brightly colored bikinis,
splashing around the surf.

Limestone Stack

Standing there,
my deformed vertical columns,
fight against, the test of time.
The wind and waves,
pound my sides.
White, foaming surf,
crash into me,
sending bubbled spray flying,
in all directions.
A full assault,
never ending.
Yet time after time,
The sights, I have seen,
of ships lost to the deep blue.
And narrow faced forms,
shimmering in the day light,
looking back at me.
I sit there, photo bombing, many selfie shots,
as my form tilts, slightly.
Rain, hail & shine,
pour down upon my tops,
gradually eroding,
my soft limestone skin.
Till I am, just a pile of rubble,
soaking among the white & blue.

Convict

Blood, tears
and sweat.
Hard labour,
built the walls.
Tiny, cold dark,
damp cells,
trapped lives in.
Sheer terror
and punishment,
endured daily.

Walls silently scream,
of the terror,
held within.
Locked away,
for life!

Only after,
can freedom,
be achieved.
Through time
and
Ticket of leave.

Quilt

Bitter cold,
early mornings.
Everyone struggles,
for a piece of quilt.
As Cassie, stretches,
pushing the quilt downwards;
uncovering everyone.
The race is on, to
scramble back, under that quilt.
Before, chilled to the bone.
Warm at last,
under the quilt.

...

Emily

Baby Emily,
snuggled up.
Fast asleep,
hanging on,
in dreamland.

Walking into Hell

Untamed monster,
unleashes havoc,
upon the dry,
sweltering land.
Breaths of intense heat,
radiates outwards;
spreading rapidly.
Flickering reddish arms,
stretches; grabbing
and devours all.
Sparks race ahead.
Fiery inferno,
ignites with burning anger.
Dark billowing plumes,
of intoxicating, dense blackness.
Houses quake in horror,
exploding from within.
Faces tremble in fear.
Suffocating gases,
smothers lives out.

Firie Gladiators

Band of the courageous crew,
taming the raging beast, within.
Firie gladiators, bestow;
volunteering battalions.
To the front lines, of waring monsters.
The fire tamers, ride,
upon their white chariots.

Dressed in golden armour,
to ward off dangerous claws.
Crowned with helmets of valor,
upon their heads.

Selfless acts of bravery.
Putting their own lives,
on the line, for others.
Protecting what is not, theirs,
before thinking of themselves.

Wielding their liquid swords,
the monster's forced to yield.
Strong brigades; take a stand,
holding the monster at bay.
Their worth, is more,
than they are paid!

Humble Dummy

Soft rubber,
held in the mouth.
Great comforter,
crunched by teeth.
Chomped and chewed,
death comes too soon.

Life, sucked out,
mangled and flat.
Sucked in,
popped out.
White, pink or blue,
small to large.
Dumped in the bin.

Drizzle

Soft as the morning dew.
So gentle, as it falls to the ground.
Even sometimes very misty.
Streaming down, like silver specks,
not even flooding, the ground.
Drizzle falls from the heavens, above.

...

Peaceful River

Dark is the night.
Stars sparkle,
upon the calm river.
The splashing of fish,
the hissing of mosquitoes.
Hot lazy days
and
cool breezy nights.

Wild

Running wild,
running free.
A great, river to be.
Weeping willows,
on the shore.
In their masses,
ready for war.

...

Rhythmical Sounds

Rhythmical sounds,
of the pinging and pong.
Smashing, against the windscreen.
Driving through,
swarming clouds.
Jumping, head on,
bodies splattering.
Crashing, banging loudly,
wings flapping.
Plague proportions.
movable roadway,
springs into action.
Windscreen changing,
from clear,
to green.

Carnage on the Windscreen

Wings flapping,
in the breeze.
Legs flying,
in all directions.
Heavy showers,
of pounding locusts.
Bashing, head first,
on to moving cars.
Freshly painted windscreens,
splattered with,
tiny brains.
Window wipers, coated,
in remains.

...

The Tumble Weed

Dry; brown, tumble weed.
Stiff, thin branches,
crackles, as it moves.
Tumbles in the wind,
stopping for a while.
Then tumbles on again.

Road Lines

Travels, forever and a day.
Never, seems to go away.
Always there,
line after line,
dot after dot.

Sleep

All quiet, inside.
Birds chirp outside.
Dim light, seeps in.
Symphony of breathing,
rises, from the quietness.

Soft hums,
waffles upwards.
From the bed,
from under the quilt.

Little, Emily's singing,
in her sleep.
Baby Cassie's,
deep in Lar, Lar land.
Eyes firmly shut,
mouth wide open.

Victor Tram

Riding along, on the,
Victor Tram.
Up the top,
the view, is grand.
As the horses trot,
along the track.
From Granite,
to the shore.

Mouse

Little, chomping teeth,
nibbling away.
Beady little eyes,
looking for movement.

Tiny pink feet,
ready to run.
Quietly waiting,
for loads more fun.

Rustling of paper,
from a narrow,
long tail.

Dainty whiskers, flicker,
from a wiggling, pink nose.
Small rounded ears,
stand to attention.

Grey furry coat,
shakes nervously.
For the not, so quiet,
as a mouse.

My home's among,

crystal clear rock pools,

down, by the sea shore.

I hide under rocks

and in crevasses.

I am small

and camouflaged.

I can be pretty to touch,

but I hold; a deadly secret.

When objects and hands,

come near me,

I splart out danger,

in brightly; colored circles.

Stay away!

My sting, is a killer.

My eight legs,

wrap around objects.

And

I'm a tiny killer.

Blue Ringed Octopus

Burned

Tender skin,
touched too close.
Skin red raw,
burned and sore.
Healing cream,
slowly healing.
Layers forming,
shiny film.
Outer scab,
in crusting.
Day by day,
fading away.

Sound Asleep

Long dark lashes,
flicker on upper cheeks.
Soft relaxed breath,
ease in and out.

Slight flickering lips,
holds the dummy in.
Heavy little arms,
lay up near, her head.

Baby Emily, sleeping,
the morning away.

First Steps

First steps,
shaking legs.
Climb up,
to standing.

Wobbly body,
staggering; hesitating step.
Falling down!
Climbing back up and holding on.

Take a step,
along the chair.
Two steps,
nearly there.
Three steps,
up and walking.

Life

Life growing,
deep inside.
Life changing,
all a round.
Only weeks old,
still forming.
Blood pumping,
over-whelming,
little life.

Hands

Little hands, study shapes.
Touching lumps, exploring life.
Clapping hands, pointing fingers,
scratching nails.
Holding bottles, feeling sensations.
Tiny finger prints.

Teeth

Big, nasty teeth,
no fun at all.
Moving up and down.
Leaving little ones,
not happy at all.
Tears are flowing,
down the face.
Not knowing,
what the teeth,
are doing.

Suzy

Bright eyed Suzy.
Such a little lady,
eats, daffodils and daisies.
On rainy afternoons.

On the Shore

Sitting on the shore,
watching the waves,
tumble by.
As the sun sets,
in the sky.

I want More

Stamping her feet!
Eyes are sparkling,
grinning ear to ear.
Hands open,
stretching out, reaching for more,
longing, hoping to receive.
Excitedly whispering,
I want more.

Little Water Baby

Tiny bathers,
clad the wet, warm body.
Pink and blue goggles,
cling to beaming eyes.
Little legs, kick backwards,
through the water.
Little cheeks,
puff in and out.
Skinny arms,
held up, with bright red,
enlarged floaties.

Little Bears

Little bears following
one by one,
through the woods, for the day.
Climbing trees, on their way.
Lots of honey,
swarms of bees.

The Water Pixie

Dancing upon,
the drops of rain.
Pitter-Patter, pattering,
down the pane.
Dressed in sparkling,
drops of dew;
with eyes of pure blue.

Drenched in golden hair
and dripping, with crystal curls.

She splashes among,
the puddles and pools.
Causing more showers,
to fall.

The Eagle

Wings, spread wide,
wind lifting them higher.
Fluffing the feathers,
as it blows past.
Gliding closer,
claws stretched.
Paused, ready,
to snatch the prey.

Seizing the moment,
eyes focused.
Head alert
and stiff.
Background blurred,
as the eagle,
speeds past.

The Ball

I'm tossed in.
They all fight,
to have me.
I'm tossed to another,
dragged through the mud.
Kicked into the air,
crashing to the ground.
Only to be chased,
time after time.
For the glory,
of flying through,
the two white poles.
And yet they, treat me,
as if I'm just another,
football.

Snuggle Time

Cassie, soundly sleeps,
sucking her pink dummy.
Fingers twitch,
as the chatter boxes,
fight over cheese crackers.
Heavy sighs, rise from Cassie,
as she dreams.
Suddenly; she stretches.
Opens one eye,
scans the room.
Then opens the other,
to look for mummy.
Found her; can be seen,
in Cassie's eyes.
She, heads straight for Mum,
for a snuggle cuddle.
Before sitting up
and staring at the TV
in amazement.

Feeding Time

Cries of hunger, fills the room.
Amazing bottle, full and ready.
Hands clenched,
down to business.
Eyes fixed and gazing.
Madly sucking,
liquid flowing.
Filling that hunger.
Sitting;
hands waving,
back, softly being tapped.
Waiting, slowly raising,
bubbles released.
Tiny hands;
sucking motion, where's more.
Finally satisfied,
tiny plays.
All that hard work,
fallen asleep.

I pong really bad.
I'm not liked by many.
I leave a bad odor,
as I go to work.
There's caution, marked,
all over me.
Brushes dip into me.
I'm spread all about.
As I dry, I bubble away.
Paint leaves, when I'm around.
I'm scraped up,
wiped onto paper.
Then I'm tossed in the bin...

Paint Stripper

Bald Eagle

Soaring high,
in the sky.
The eagle hovers,
above my eye.
Flying free, for,
us to see.

Jane Eliza Landing

Jane Eliza Landing,
peaceful the surroundings.
Happy red gums, standing,
along the shoreline.
Paddle wheels, are turning,
water is flying.
The Liba Fleet's traveling,
up and down the river.
On and off sandbars,
all day long.

Old Bright Eyes

Old Bright Eyes,
looking down.

The new face,
full of dimples.

A strongman's,
power,
moving waters.

Always there,
shining brightly.
Brighter than,
the stars.

A quarterly smile,
ready to play,
peek a boo.

Light's A Blazing

Monstrous trucks,
rolling down the road,
rumbling, on in.
Disturbing the peace,
as you; lay there sleeping.
Light's a blazing!
Displaying,
like Christmas trees,
on wheels.

Traveling slowly about,
my silvery, paths are left,
behind.
Small and meek,
that I am.
Even, the kitchen sink!
Is packed away,
in my house;
on my back.

Snail

My Heart

My heart is breaking!
For my little,
black eyed beauty.
Salty rain, rolls down,
my face.
Sweet Zoe, goodbye,
my love.

Raining from the Eyelids

Missing, those tiny,
dainty feet.
Prancing, dancing,
as you run, excitedly;
up to me.
Water wells up; pooling,
at the bottom; of my eyes.
Rain starts to pour,
dripping; from the eyelids.

Bugga, More Pain

Lying there;
belly resting upon a,
flattened pillow.
Arms and legs,
move about, from within.

Still, I am,
so uncomfortable.
Muscle and bone,
ache in all directions.
Struggling to sit up,
pain over - powering.

Holding on,
slowly raising; to stand.
One step, at a time,
waddling forwards,
arriving at last.

The toilet is near,
turning; stepping slowly,
finally sitting;
still uncomfortable.

Cont. >

Waiting; thinking,
waiting some more.

Wasted effect,
only a few drops.
Struggling back up,
to standing, on my feet.
Waddling back to the bedroom,
like an over grown fat duck.
Clamber back into bed,
arranging the pillows to just right.
Heavy breathing,
semi-comfortable,
not happy at all.

A sigh, of relief; fills my face,
while, pulling the covers up,
over all lumps and bumps.
Rest at last!
Oh no..
The toilet, calls again.

Bug's Tea Party

Dashing medley; as they go,
in their best dresses; for the show.
Bugs dancing, to the disco.
Of the sparkling, beaming lights.
Spiraling out of control,
round and round,
they go.

At the Summer Fair

Little Meggy Sue, lost,
poor baby, Jimmy Brown,
at the summer fair.
With his hair of golden curls
and eyes of sky blue.

Meggy Sue, looked everywhere!
Baby, Jimmy Brown,
was nowhere, to be found!

But then..
She, slowly looked up,
with her mouth, wide open.
There was Jimmy Brown!

Riding, round and round,
on the big red tractor.

Wally

Along the shady, creek bed,
down among the gum trees.
Wally, sits and waits; thinking,
while chewing, on gum leaves.

Along comes Con, the catfish,
saying, catch me; if you can.

So Wally, puts his hand in
and pulls, him out again.

Con, the catfish,
whispers, shaking.
Please; put me back.
And please; don't munch,
on me.
Like you did,
last week.

Weather Man

Weather man, said.
Have no fear,
it wont rain, a drop.
And down it came,
drop after drop
and it didn't stop.
Flooding garden beds
and pouring down drains.
Soaking dry washing,
on the lines.

Storm

Crashing; booms roll down,
from above.
Glimmering flashes; of white,
streaks, across the sky.
Booming; rumblings,
seep through trees.

Sick

Raging heat wave;
soaring temperatures,
body burning up.
Heavy laden,
struggling, breath.
Little eyes staring out,
must keep fluids up.

few wet nappies; in between,
fighting hands, pushing bottle away.

Blocked runny nose;
mouth open, gasping for air.

Droplets of liquid,
slowly fall, in mouth opening.
Forced to swallow,
medicine;
finally in!
Peace at last,
baby sleeping.

Miss Hothead

Little Miss Hothead,
fumbling among the thorns.
Grumbling at everything,
that comes her way.
In her; little green,
frog slippers.
Tip toeing, too and fro.
Eating, rose petals,
in her path.
And reaching for more,
along the way.
Leaving crumbs,
trailing,
behind her.

Little Sleepy Head

Early morning rise,
crisp, is the new born day.
Bird's chattering,
Kookaburra's laughing.
Johnathon's sleeping,
the morning away.

Tired

Tiny bombshell,
racing round.
Unrested soul,
overtired brain.
Unwilling to stop,
little tantrums, show through.

The tell tail signs,
the body's in pain.
Legs give way,
unable to stand.

Slowly, giving up,
arms, flop down.
Eyes struggle to stay awake,
finally curling up.
Eyes shut,
in sleeping slumber.

Tears

Slowly, water wells up,
in sad; hazel eyes.
Eyelashes become,
wet and heavy;
till over flowing.
Round balls of liquid;
rolling down,
tender, pink cheeks.
Dripping from the,
lower chin line.
Salty tear droplets;
fall,
splashing on the paper.
Spreading, as it hits,
smudging ink,
as it soaks in.

The Grumble Bear

Lips pout,
while eyebrows frown.
Not happy looks,
growling anger.
Crying; wailing,
sobs everywhere.
Legs kick,
madly about.
Face screwed up,
Amy, the grumble bear.

The Cranky Old Lady

The cranky old lady,
across the road.
Yells; all day long,
at the littlest, of things.

She bellows,
it out!
With an anger,
so great.

At the top; of her voice,
for all to hear.

No peace and quiet,
will be achieved.
When,
that cranky old lady.

Wakes from her sleep!

Weeping Willows

The weeping, Willows,
weep all day,
with the charm, of yesterday.
Hanging there, in the breeze,
with not a care, for other trees.

The Change

The wind blows
and leaves shake.
Trembling; in the breeze.
Dust flies about
and dark stormy clouds,
fills the sky.
The approaching change,
is on it's way.

Stress

Stress; worry,
go hand in hand.
Tiredness; up all night,
with my tiny Love.
Eyes hanging out,
longing for some sleep.
Baby rolling,
legs and arms; flapping around.
Little body; back and forth,
tossing about;
baby burning up.
Cold wet towels,
lay scrunched up.
Lots of tears
and many hours,
of restless; crying.
Finally,
heavy snoring.
Time to rest;
while watching,
the sun; come up.

Little Ones

From tiny;
Pitter-patter, pattering feet,
to rumbling; foot steps.
Small voices,
echo, through the air.
Heat from the box,
slowly warms the room.
Eyes glued; in place,
still as a mouse.
Watching the show,
go by.

Grandma's

Are full of fun,
for little ones.
Loves to hug,
sad, wet eyes.
Cheers little red,
cheeks.

Twins

Two peas in a pod.
The same,
but yet different.
Cute as a button,
one girl, one boy.
Stuck together,
yet, can be apart.

Puppy

Dancing; prancing,
ball of fluff.
Hopping; popping,
cuddly and soft.
Boing here, boing there,
little mischief everywhere.
Wet sloppy, chew toys,
slimy, under foot.

The Grand Old Lady

One hundred year's young,
the Grand Old Lady, lying still;
in the blackness of time.

Her great hull, standing silent,
weeping for it's precious cargo.

Shivering, vaporous forms,
of first class and steerage;
stroll hand in hand, together to the,
surging currents, of the Atlantic.

A vast wardrobe; of scattered luggage,
across the sandy floor.

Small ghostly forms; play chase y,
among,
the tattered decks.

Fear in the Hearts

Gray, streamlined body, moves swiftly;
through the blue waters.

Black glassy eyes,
stare deep; into your soul.

Sharp serrated teeth;
grinning in anticipation.
Gums lunging forward,
as the mouth; widens,
in a chomping motion.

Eyes roll to white,
in the attack!

White pointer; snout,
nudges the prey.

Triengler fins; slice,
through the surface.
Sending terror;
in the eyes, of swimmers,
fear; in the hearts and minds.

Content

About the Author

Jacquelyn, wrote her first poem, On the Shore; way back in 1977, while working on a class project, where She and her fellow class mate, had their finished poems publish in a small book; titled Opinions.
Jacquelyn, found her class teacher, Mrs McKay, to be a great inspiration and continued to carry on writing.
These days She continues to write, she also enjoys photography, genealogy & craft making.

Other Books the author has written are

Tasmania's Cradle
Love Hurts
Provoking the Senses
Touch of Sunshine
132 Ways to Make your Heart Fly

Books are available from
http://au.blurb.com/user/store/Ecaabooks

Notes